D0608021

Contents

CREDITS

EDITOR: Wendy Slotboom
COPY EDITOR: Laurie Shifrin
ILLUSTRATIONS AND BOOK DESIGN:
Wendy Slotboom and
Marsha McCloskey
COVER DESIGN: Jason Yenter
PHOTOGRAPHY: Ken Wagner
PHOTO STYLING: Sharon Yenter

Fat 8ths and Friends
©2006 Marsha McCloskey
In The Beginning, Seattle, Washington USA

ISBN: 0-9706900-6-1
Printed in USA

Introduction

When my mother was married in 1943, the wedding present from her grandmother was a scrap quilt. The pattern is made of 60° diamonds arranged in six-pointed stars. My mother remembers the fabrics in the center of the quilt as being from summer dresses that were made for the three girls in the family.

In the 1930s and 40s, the time of the Great Depression and World War II, quilters used scraps out of necessity. Popular patterns from this era were characterized by the use of many different prints. Patterns were published in newspapers and were eagerly collected. Most of the colors of the 1930's prints were muted pastels, but as the 1940s arrived, the colors became bolder and brighter. The printing technology changed and the prints also became larger and more flamboyant.

During the war, women were encouraged to "make do." Fabric was dear and some feed and flour companies put their products in printed cloth sacks to promote sales. Quilters used these feedsacks, as well as leftovers from dressmaking, and salvaged parts of worn-out garments in their work. Quilts were made for bed covers and charity fund raisers, and were also a source of income for cash-strapped families. I imagine the making of the quilts was a strong antidote to the harsh times, a positive endeavor with both personal and social rewards.

Now, in the 21st century, the collective memory of previous hard times is fading. What we see is the charm of the quilts and fabrics of the 1930s and 40s, and we associate them with our family histories. When I talk to non-quilters about what I do, inevitably they will tell me about warm childhood memories of quilts and their grandmothers.

When there is too much going on in my life to concentrate on elaborate quilt designs, I gravitate to simple patterns and bright colors. The reproduction fabrics from my mother's youth fit the bill perfectly. There is great comfort in just putting my hands on cloth, experiencing the color and the rhythm of sewing. I suspect that women have always felt that way about their quilting. An activity that looks like work is also the source of personal entertainment and great satisfaction. I hope you enjoy working with the fabrics and quilt designs in *Fat 8ths and Friends* as much as I have.

Marsha McCloskey

Getting Started

ALL ABOUT FAT 8THS

Fat 8ths and Friends is a collection of six quilt patterns made with reproduction prints from the 1930s and 1940s. These scrappy quilt patterns use a variety of prints and are written for Fat 8ths, or pieces of fabric that measure $10^{1/2}$" x 18".

Quilt stores often sell precut fat quarter yards, measuring 18" x 21", either one at a time or in coordinated packets. Quilters like them because they provide more useable fabric than quarter yards measured off the bolt at 9". Likewise, a Fat 8th yard allows more useable fabric than a $4^{1/2}$" strip cut from the bolt. Most quilt stores will not even cut eighths because of the awkward shape of the pieces. Fat 8ths are sometimes offered in 9" x 21" pieces, but we've found those pieces to be less useful that the $10^{1/2}$" x 18" cuts. By simply cutting fat quarters in half the short way, quilt shops can offer Fat 8ths and provide quilters with a nice selection of prints in this smaller format.

In The Beginning Fabrics is now printing four prints on the same bolt with each print running in a lengthwise stripe (parallel to the selvage) that measures $10^{1/2}$" wide. Cut a half yard (18") from the bolt, then cut the prints apart and you have four coordinated Fat 8ths! It's a great way to get a wide variety of prints for your collection for not a lot of money.

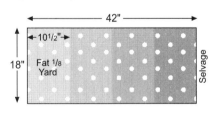

If your fabric is not printed with 4 different prints, you can still cut Fat 8ths. Cut a half yard of fabric (18" x 42"); then divide the half yard in half to make 2 "fat" quarter yards, each measuring 18" x 21". Then divide each fat quarter in half the short way to make 4 Fat 8ths, each measuring $10^{1/2}$" x 18".

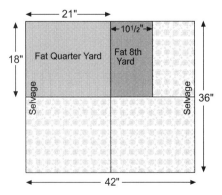

The "Friends" in the book title refers to the additional yardage that is inevitably needed to make a quilt. In the *Fat 8ths and Friends* fabric collection, there are several coordinating fabrics that are printed just one design on the bolt. These larger pieces are intended for borders, setting pieces, backings, and bindings.

Fat 8th Yields

To prepare my fabric, I rinse it in warm water and dry it in the dryer. I do this before cutting for three reasons: to check for color fastness, to preshrink, and to "rough-up" the surface so that patches don't slip during piecing.

To allow for cutting variations and shrinkage, Fat 8th yields are based on a useable 10" x 17" piece of fabric (ideally $10^{1/2}$" x 18"). After rinsing, drying, and pressing your Fat 8ths, measure the pieces. If there is not a useable 10" x 17", you may need to buy more fabric. If your piece of fabric is more generous, you may be able to cut more patches than are shown in the diagrams.

Quiltmaking Basics:

CUTTING AND PIECING

Rotary Cutting

The basic tools for cutting fabric patches are a rotary cutter, ruler, and mat. If you don't already own rotary cutting tools, choose a cutter that fits comfortably in your hand, a self-healing mat, and an acrylic ruler that measures at least 6" x 24" and is marked with measurements in $1/4$" and $1/8$" increments.

If you are new to rotary cutting, practice on scrap fabric first. The blade is very sharp; it is not necessary to press very hard when you first begin, but be sure to place even pressure on the blade as you cut. Always remember to: keep your fingers and other body parts away from the blade, close the blade each time you finish cutting, and keep the cutter out of the reach of children. The cutter can be dangerous if not used with proper care.

Cutting Strips from Yardage

Fold the fabric selvage to selvage, aligning the widthwise and lengthwise grains as best you can.

Place fabric on the rotary cutting mat with the folded edge closest to you. Align a square plastic cutting ruler with the fold of the fabric and place a long cutting ruler to the left.

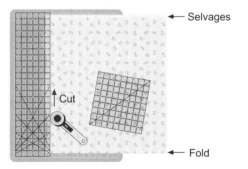

When making all cuts, fabric should be placed to your right. (If you are left handed, reverse the directions.) Remove the square plastic ruler and make a rotary cut along the right side of the long ruler to trim away the uneven raw edges of fabric. Be sure to hold the ruler firmly in place, and roll the cutter away from you, cutting through all layers.

Make successive cuts measuring from the first cut as shown. All strips are cut with the 1/4" seam allowance included.

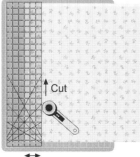

To cut border strips on lengthwise grain, position the fabric so cuts will be parallel to the selvage. Make the first cut parallel to the selvage close enough to trim it away and create a clean edge from which to measure. Make successive cuts measuring from the first cut.

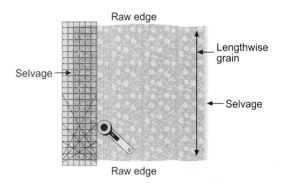

Our patterns call for cutting strips from Fat 8ths. Generally, cut the strips across the long dimension, parallel to the selvage. If more than one size strip is to be cut from the same Fat 8th, a cutting chart will be shown. Also, if strips are to be cut across the short dimension, a cutting chart will be provided.

Squares and Rectangles

Measurements given for cutting squares and rectangles include 1/4" seam allowances. First cut fabric into strips in the width given in the instructions. Using the square plastic cutting ruler, align the top and bottom edge of strip and cut fabric into squares the same width as the strip.

Cut rectangles in the same manner, first cutting strips the width of the rectangle, then cutting to the proper length.

Triangles

Cut fabric in strips, then into squares the size specified in the instructions. The measurements given for half- and quarter-square triangles in the quilt directions include $1/4$" seam allowances.

Half-Square Triangles

If you need a triangle with the straight grain on the short side, cut half-square triangles. Cut a square, then cut it in half diagonally once. The resulting two triangles will have short sides on the straight grain of the fabric and the long side on the bias.

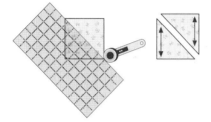

Quarter-Square Triangles

If you need a triangle with the straight grain on the long side, cut quarter-square triangles. Cut a square, then cut it in half diagonally twice. The resulting four triangles will have the long side on the straight grain and the short sides on the bias.

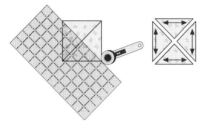

Trimming Triangle Points

Templates are provided for patches in the quilt designs. Use them to make templates for hand piecing or to check rotary-cut shapes for accuracy. Trimlines shown on triangular templates make it easy to match shapes for sewing. Use the Precision Trimmer 3 as shown to trim triangles where indicated in the quilt patterns and on the templates.

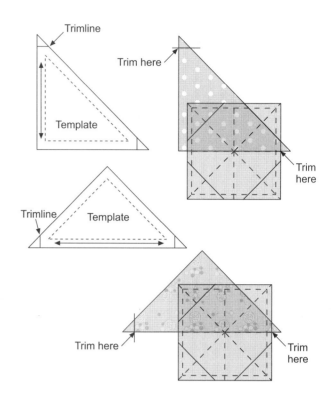

Machine Piecing

To make a pieced block, sew the smallest pieces together first to form units. Join smaller units to form larger ones until the block is complete. Diagrams with each quilt pattern show the order in which to sew the patches together.

Use 100 percent cotton thread as light as the lightest fabric in the project. Sew exact $1/4$" seams. On some machines the width of the presser foot is $1/4$" and can be used as guide. If you don't have such a foot, you'll need to establish the proper seam allowance on your sewing machine. Place a piece of quarter- or eighth-inch graph paper under the presser foot and gently lower the needle onto the line that is $1/4$" from the edge of the paper. Lay a piece of masking tape at the edge of the paper to act as the $1/4$" guide.

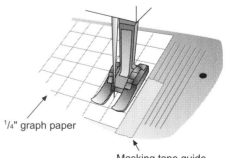

For the patterns in this book, sew from cut edge to cut edge. Backtack if you wish, but when a seam line will be crossed and held by another, it is not necessary. Use chain piecing whenever possible to save time and thread. To chain piece, sew one seam, but do not lift the presser foot. Do not take the piece out of the sewing machine and do not cut the thread. Instead, set up the next seam to be sewn and stitch as you did the first. There will be a little twist of thread between the two pieces. Sew all the seams you can at one time in this way, then remove the "chain." Clip the threads.

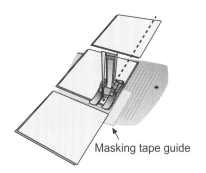

Masking tape guide

Pinning

Pin seams before stitching if matching is involved, if your seams are longer than 4", or if your fabrics are a little slippery. Pin points of matching (where seam lines or points meet) first. Once these important points are firmly in place, pin the rest of the seam, easing if necessary. Keep pins away from seam lines, as sewing over them tends to damage the needle and makes it hard to be accurate in tight places.

Pressing

In this book, most seams are pressed to one side, toward the darker fabric whenever possible. Sometimes, for matching purposes, seams are pressed in opposite directions, regardless of which is the darker fabric. Other times seams are pressed open to distribute bulk.

Press with a dry iron that has a shot of steam when needed. Take care not to overpress. First, press the sewn seam flat to "set" it. Next, press the seam open or to the side as instructed. Press from both the right and wrong sides to make the seam flat without little pleats at the ends.

ABOUT THE PATTERNS

The six quilt patterns on the following pages were designed to be easy and fun to make. If you don't like triangles, try the Wind Rows quilt on page 24. If you like simple appliqué, try the Flower Pot quilt on page 28. Willing to try a few triangles? Make Blossom Time on page 6 or Crackerbox on page 21. If you love the interplay of triangles over the surface of a quilt, then Corn and Beans, on page 14, is the design for you.

In the Materials lists, fabric requirements are given in Fat 8ths for the scrappy parts of the quilts and in normal 40"-wide yardage for most setting pieces, borders, bindings, and backings. (The 40"-wide measurement is "useable width." With selvages included, your fabric will be wider.) A fabric requirement that reads, "1 Fat 8th each of 12 or more assorted prints for blocks" means that you need to buy at least 12 different Fat 8ths to make the block designs. If you find more fabrics than 12, by all means, use them as well. Study the color photographs of the quilts found on the inside front and back covers and in the Quilt Gallery, in the center of the book, to get an idea of the variety of prints needed.

Cutting diagrams are given with each pattern to help you get the most out of every Fat 8th. First, read the information on the number of pieces to cut, then look at the Fat 8th cutting diagrams to see how to cut the necessary patches. All cutting instructions include a $1/4$" seam allowance.

Block Dimensions

Measure your sewn blocks for accuracy. When you have made a block for a quilt, it will have a "finished" dimension and an "edge-to-edge" dimension. The "finished" dimension is the measurement of the square without seam allowances, after it is sewn into the quilt. The "edge-to-edge" or raw measurement includes seam allowances and should be $1/2$" larger than the finished dimension. Finished block dimensions are given at the beginning of each pattern. You'll find edge-to-edge dimensions in the piecing instructions.

See quilt finishing instructions on pages 34-36.

Blossom Time

Sharon Yenter designed this easy-to-make pattern to showcase a variety of pastel 30's and 40's prints. Cut the shapes out of all the fabrics first, then place them on a design wall to achieve the best arrangement.

DESIGNED BY: Sharon Evans Yenter

QUILTED BY: Sherry D. Rogers

FINISHED QUILT SIZE: 53" x 64"

FINISHED BLOCK SIZE: $9^3/_8$" x $9^3/_8$"

See this quilt in color in the center of the book.

MATERIALS

Fabric requirements are based on Fat 8ths (useable measurement: 10" x 17"), or 40" fabric width.

• 1 Fat 8th *each* of 3 or more assorted solids or solid-looking prints (pinks, greens, and blues) for blocks
• 1 Fat 8th *each* of 12 assorted prints for blocks
• 1 Fat 8th *each* of 5 assorted small prints with white background for blocks
  OR $^5/_8$ yd. of one print
• 1 Fat 8th *each* of 4 assorted prints for sashing
  OR $^5/_8$ yd. cherry print
• 1 Fat 8th green print for cornerstones
• $^1/_3$ yd. dark green print for inner border
• $2^1/_2$ yds.* floral bouquet print for outer border and binding
• $3^5/_8$ yds. for backing (widthwise seam)
• 61" x 72" batting

*Yardage is generous to allow for selective placement of floral bouquet design.

DIRECTIONS

See *Quiltmaking Basics,* beginning on page 2, for general cutting and piecing directions. All cutting measurements include $^1/_4$"-wide seam allowance. Press seams in direction of arrows unless otherwise instructed.

CUTTING

When a number is followed by a second number in parentheses, the first number indicates the pieces needed to make one block. The number in parentheses indicates the pieces needed to make all 20 blocks.

From Fat 8th assortment of 3 solids (pinks, greens, and blues), cut a total of:
• 4 (80) #1 squares, 2" x 2", for blocks

Study Fat 8th cutting diagrams below and then, from Fat 8th assortment of 12 prints, cut:
- 5 (100) #1 squares, 2" x 2", for blocks
- 2 (40) #4 rectangles, 2" x $9^7/_8$", for blocks
- 2 (40) #3 rectangles, 2" x $6^7/_8$", for blocks

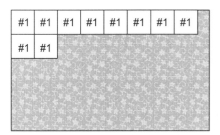

When cut as shown, one Fat 8th will yield eight #1 squares, four #3 rectangles, and four #4 rectangles. Do this with 10 of the Fat 8ths.

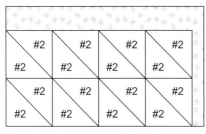

Cut ten #1 squares from each of the remaining 2 Fat 8ths.

From Fat 8th assortment of 5 small prints with white background, or from $^5/_8$ yd. piece, cut:
- 2 (40) squares, 4" x 4"; cut each square once diagonally to make 4 (80) #2 triangles for blocks. Trim points for easy matching using Precision Trimmer 3 as shown on page 4, referring to the trimlines on the #2 triangle template on page 9.

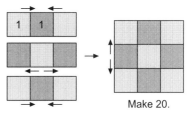

When cut as shown, one Fat 8th will yield 16 #2 triangles. Do this 5 times.

From Fat 8th assortment of 4 prints, or from $^5/_8$ yd. cherry print, cut:
- 31 #4 rectangles, 2" x $9^7/_8$", for sashing

When cut as shown, one Fat 8th will yield eight #4 rectangles. Do this 4 times. You will have 1 extra rectangle.

From green print, cut:
- 12 #1 squares, 2" x 2", for cornerstones

From dark green print, cut:
- 5 strips, $1^1/_4$" x 40", for inner border

From floral bouquet print, cut in order given:
- 7 strips, $2^1/_2$" x 40", for double-fold binding
- 4 lengthwise strips, 67" x 5" wide, for outer border (Strips are cut long to allow for selective placement of floral bouquets.)

BLOCK ASSEMBLY
1. Using 4 solid #1 squares and 5 assorted print #1 squares, assemble 1 ninepatch as shown. Edge-to-edge measurement of ninepatch should be 5". Repeat to make 20 ninepatches.

Make 20.

2. Sew 4 assorted small print #2 triangles to 1 ninepatch. Edge-to-edge measurement of unit should be $6^7/8$". Repeat to make 20 units.

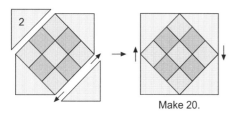

Make 20.

3. Add 2 assorted print #3 rectangles and 2 assorted print #4 rectangles to 1 unit as shown. Edge-to-edge measurement of block should be $9^7/8$". Repeat to make 20 blocks.

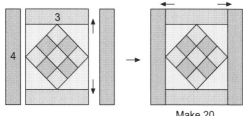

Make 20.

QUILT TOP ASSEMBLY

1. Using blocks, sashing strips, and cornerstone squares, assemble 5 of Row A, and 4 of Row B as shown.

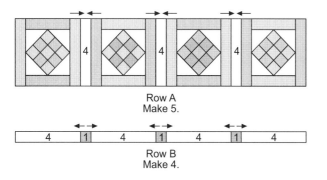

Row A
Make 5.

Row B
Make 4.

2. Sew rows together as shown in the Quilt Assembly Diagram at right. Press seams toward sashing rows.

BORDERS

1. Sew the 5 dark green border strips together, end-to-end, to make one long strip. Press seams open.

2. Measure length of quilt top through center. From the long strip, cut 2 dark green border strips to this measurement, and sew to sides of quilt. Press seams toward border.

3. Measure width of quilt top, including borders just added, through center. From the long strip, cut 2 dark green border strips to this measurement, and sew to top and bottom of quilt. Press seams toward border.

4. Place 2 of the floral bouquet border strips next to sides of quilt top and, paying particular attention to corners, decide on placement of the bouquets. Trim the 2 border strips to size, and sew to sides of quilt. Press seams toward floral bouquet border.

5. Place 2 remaining floral bouquet border strips at top and bottom of quilt top. When satisfied with placement of bouquets, trim the border strips to size, and sew to quilt. Press seams toward floral bouquet border.

Quilt Assembly Diagram

See finishing instructions on pages 34-36.

Templates

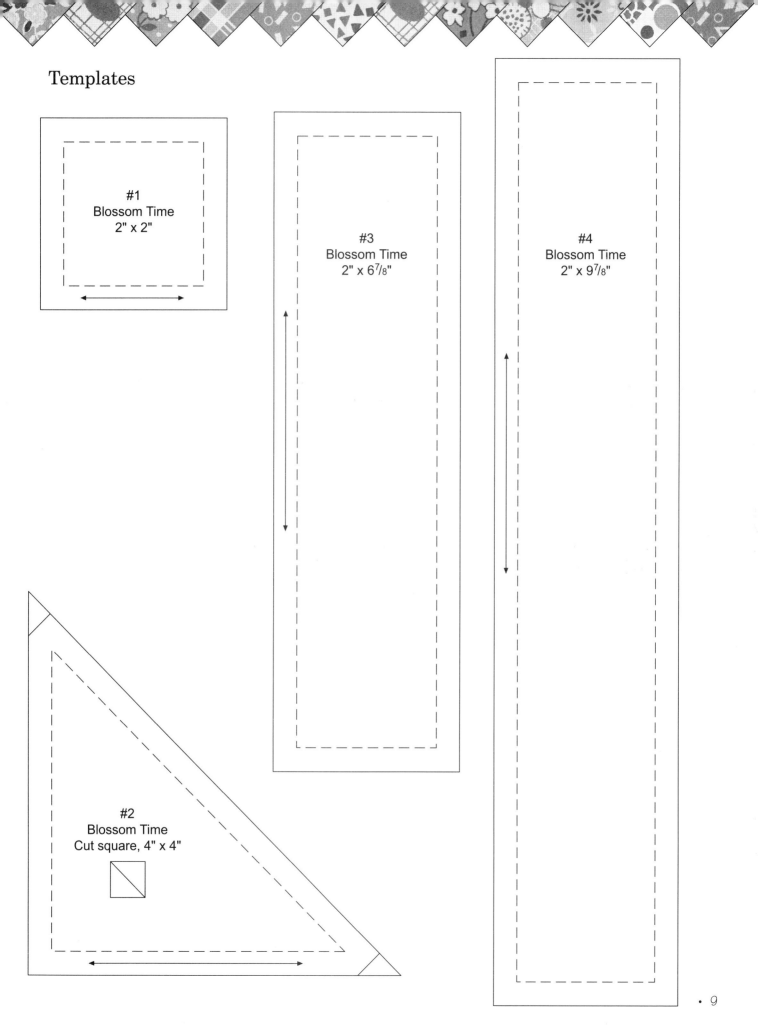

#1
Blossom Time
2" x 2"

#3
Blossom Time
2" x 6$\frac{7}{8}$"

#4
Blossom Time
2" x 9$\frac{7}{8}$"

#2
Blossom Time
Cut square, 4" x 4"

Flying High

The design for the Flying High quilt is based on a pieced airplane block from the Carrie Hall collection of patchwork designs dating from the 1930s. Reproduction prints from the 30s and 40s in primary colors make a lively and whimsical little quilt.

DESIGNED BY: Marsha McCloskey

QUILTED BY: Margy Duncan

FINISHED QUILT SIZE: 42$\frac{1}{2}$" x 44$\frac{1}{2}$"

FINISHED BLOCK SIZE: 10" x 10"

See this quilt in color on the inside back cover.

MATERIALS

Fabric requirements are based on Fat 8ths (useable measurement: 10" x 17"), or 40" fabric width.

- 1 Fat 8th *each* of 12 or more assorted colored prints for blocks and borders
- 1 Fat 8th *each* of 9 or more assorted light prints for blocks
- $\frac{1}{2}$ yd. blue tonal for binding
- 3 yds. for backing
- 51" x 53" batting

DIRECTIONS

See *Quiltmaking Basics*, beginning on page 2, for general cutting and piecing directions. All cutting measurements include $\frac{1}{4}$"-wide seam allowance. Press seams in direction of arrows unless otherwise instructed.

CUTTING

When a number is followed by a second number in parentheses, the first number indicates the pieces needed to make one block. The number in parentheses indicates the pieces needed to make all 9 blocks.

Study Fat 8th Cutting Diagrams below and then, from Fat 8th assortment of 12 colored prints, cut a total of:
- 28 strips, $2^1/2$" x 17", for borders
- 1 (9) #6 triangles for blocks (use template)
- 1 (9) squares, $3^1/4$" x $3^1/4$"; cut each square twice diagonally to make 4 (36) #2 triangles for blocks (You will use 18 of the triangles; trim points for easy matching, referring to the trimlines on the #2 triangle template on page 13.)
- 1 (9) #5 rectangles, $2^1/2$" x $6^1/2$", for blocks
- 4 (36) #4 squares, $2^1/2$" x $2^1/2$", for blocks
- 18 #4 squares, $2^1/2$" x $2^1/2$", for setting units and borders

Study Fat 8th Cutting Diagram below and then, from Fat 8th assortment of 9 light prints, cut a total of:
- 2 (18) squares, $1^7/8$" x $1^7/8$"; cut each square once diagonally to make 4 (36) #1 triangles for blocks (Trim points for easy matching, referring to the trimlines on the #1 triangle template on page 13.)
- 2 (18) #3 rectangles, $1^1/2$" x $2^1/2$", for blocks
- 1 + 1 reversed (9 + 9 reversed) #7 triangles for blocks (use template)
- 2 (18) #4 squares, $2^1/2$" x $2^1/2$", for blocks
- 9 #4 squares, $2^1/2$" x $2^1/2$", for setting units
- 4 (36) #5 rectangles, $2^1/2$" x $6^1/2$", for blocks

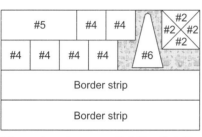

When cut as shown, one Fat 8th will yield 2 border strips, four #2 triangles, six #4 squares, one #5 rectangle, and one #6 triangle. Do this 9 times, once for each block.

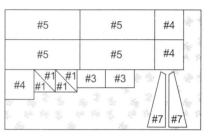

When cut as shown, one Fat 8th will yield four #1 triangles, two #3 rectangles, three #4 squares, four #5 rectangles, and two #7 triangles. Do this 9 times, once for each block.

From blue tonal, cut:
- 5 strips, $2^1/2$" x 40", for double-fold binding

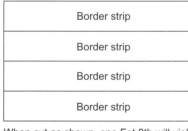

When cut as shown, one Fat 8th will yield 4 border strips. Do this 3 times. Only 10 strips are needed.

BLOCK ASSEMBLY

1. Before assembling blocks, refer to photo on inside back cover for color placement. Then make 9 airplane blocks as shown. Edge-to-edge measurement of block should be $10^{1}/_{2}$" x $10^{1}/_{2}$".

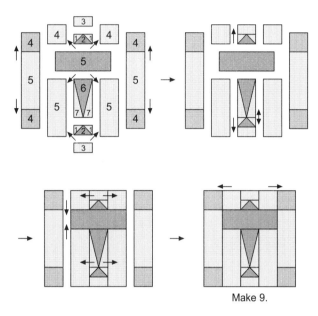

Make 9.

QUILT TOP ASSEMBLY

1. Using 3 light print #4 squares, and 2 colored print # 4 squares, assemble 1 setting unit as shown. Repeat to make 3 setting units.

Make 3.

2. Using airplane blocks and setting units, make 3 vertical rows as shown.

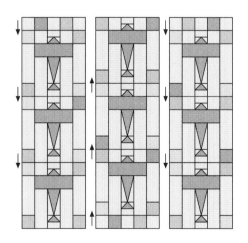

3. Sew rows together as shown in the Quilt Assembly Diagram below. Press seams in one direction.

BORDERS

1. Sew the colored print $2^{1}/_{2}$" x 17" border strips together, end-to-end, to make one long strip. Press seams open.

2. Border 1: Measure width of quilt top through center. From the long strip, cut 2 border strips to this measurement. Add a colored print #4 square to each end of these 2 border strips. Press seams away from #4 squares. Set these border strips aside. Measure length of quilt top through center. From the long strip, cut 2 border strips to this measurement and sew to sides of quilt. Press seams toward border. Sew the set-aside border strips to top and bottom of quilt. Press seams toward border.

3. Borders 2 and 3: Repeat Step 2 twice more to make the remaining borders.

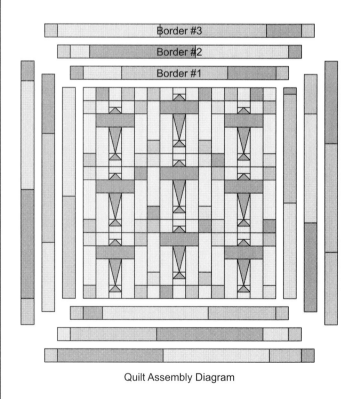

Quilt Assembly Diagram

See finishing instructions on pages 34-36.

Templates

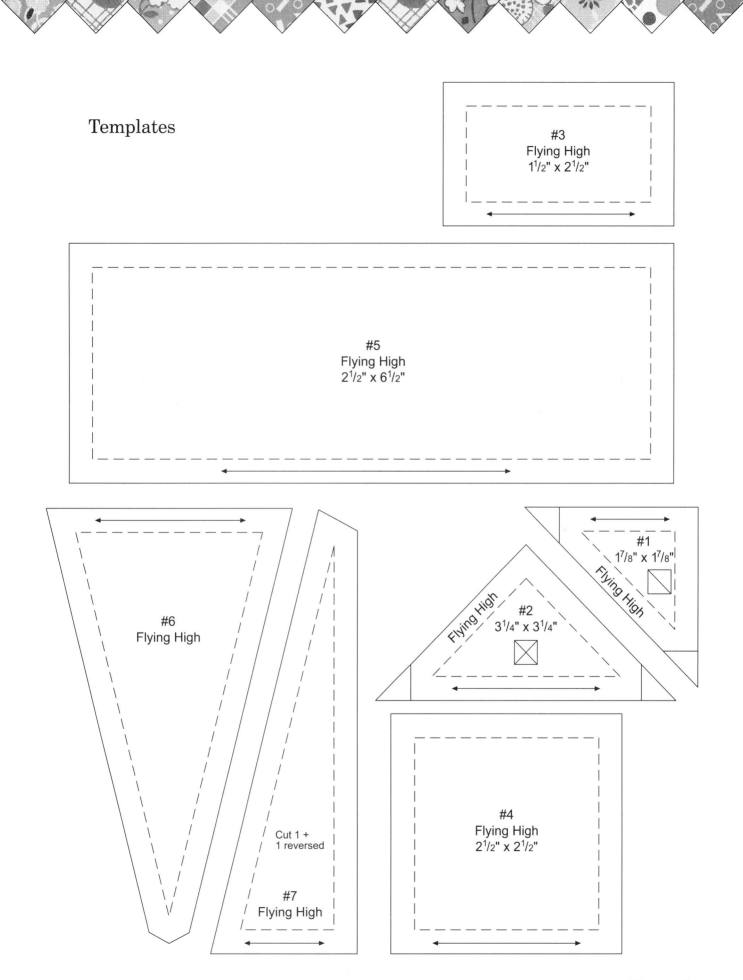

#3
Flying High
$1^1/_2$" x $2^1/_2$"

#5
Flying High
$2^1/_2$" x $6^1/_2$"

#6
Flying High

#1
$1^7/_8$" x $1^7/_8$"
Flying High

Flying High

#2
$3^1/_4$" x $3^1/_4$"

Cut 1 +
1 reversed

#7
Flying High

#4
Flying High
$2^1/_2$" x $2^1/_2$"

Corn and Beans

Corn and Beans is the traditional name for this design. In the early 20th century, it was always made with yellow and green on a muslin ground. Adding the pink and purple pinwheels to the coloring livens it up a bit.

DESIGNED BY: Marsha McCloskey

QUILTED BY: Carrie Peterson

FINISHED QUILT SIZE: 48$\frac{1}{2}$" x 60$\frac{1}{2}$"

FINISHED BLOCK SIZE: 6" x 6"

See this quilt in color in the center of the book.

MATERIALS

Fabric requirements are based on Fat 8ths (useable measurement: 10" x 17"), or 40" fabric width.

- 1 Fat 8th *each* of 2 or more assorted green prints for blocks (we used 1 print)
- 1 Fat 8th *each* of 2 or more assorted purple prints for blocks (we used 1 print)
- 1 Fat 8th *each* of 2 or more assorted pink prints for blocks (we used 1 print)
- 1 Fat 8th *each* of 2 or more assorted lavender prints for blocks (we used 1 print)
- 1 Fat 8th *each* of 8 or more assorted medium-scale prints for blocks (we used 2 fat 8ths each of 4 prints)
- 1 Fat 8th *each* of 7 or more assorted small-scale light prints for blocks (we used 2 fat 8ths each of 4 prints)
- 1$\frac{1}{2}$ yds. pink plaid for inner border
- 1$\frac{3}{4}$ yds. large-scale yellow floral for outer border and blocks
- $\frac{5}{8}$ yd. yellow tonal for binding
- 3$\frac{3}{8}$ yds. for backing (widthwise seam)
- 57" x 69" batting

DIRECTIONS

See *Quiltmaking Basics,* beginning on page 2, for general cutting and piecing directions. All cutting measurements include $\frac{1}{4}$"-wide seam allowance. Press seams in direction of arrows unless otherwise instructed.

CUTTING

When a number is followed by a second number in parentheses, the first number indicates the pieces needed to make one block. The number in parentheses indicates the pieces needed to make all 48 blocks.

From Fat 8th assortment of 2 or more green prints, cut:
- 1 (24) squares, 2⅞" x 2⅞"; cut each square once diagonally to make 2 (48) #1 triangles for blocks

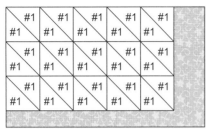

When cut as shown, one Fat 8th will yield thirty #1 triangles.

From Fat 8th assortment of 2 or more purple prints, cut:
- 1 (24) squares, 2⅞" x 2⅞"; cut each square once diagonally to make 2 (48) #1 triangles for blocks

From Fat 8th assortment of 2 or more pink prints, cut:
- 1 (24) squares, 2⅞" x 2⅞"; cut each square once diagonally to make 2 (48) #1 triangles for blocks (only one triangle is needed for each block)

From Fat 8th assortment of 2 or more lavender prints, cut:
- 1 (24) squares, 2⅞" x 2⅞"; cut each square once diagonally to make 2 (48) #1 triangles for blocks (only one triangle is needed for each block)

From Fat 8th assortment of 8 or more medium-scale prints, cut:
- 1 (24) squares, 4⅞" x 4⅞"; cut each square once diagonally to make 2 (48) #2 triangles for blocks (only one triangle is needed for each block)
- 1 (24) squares, 2⅞" x 2⅞"; cut each square once diagonally to make 2 (48) #1 triangles for blocks (only one triangle is needed for each block)

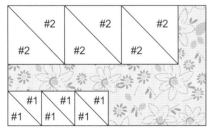

When cut as shown, one Fat 8th will yield six #2 triangles, and six #1 triangles.

From Fat 8th assortment of 7 or more small-scale light prints, cut:
- 2 (96) squares, 2⅞" x 2⅞"; cut each square once diagonally to make 4 (192) #1 triangles for blocks

From pink plaid, cut:
- 4 strips, the length* of fabric x 4½" wide, for inner border

From large-scale yellow floral, cut in order given:
- 4 strips, the length* of fabric x 2½" wide, for outer border
- 1 (24) squares, 4⅞" x 4⅞"; cut each square once diagonally to make 2 (48) #2 triangles for blocks (only one triangle is needed for each block)
- 1 (24) squares, 2⅞" x 2⅞"; cut each square once diagonally to make 2 (48) #1 triangles for blocks (only one triangle is needed for each block)

From yellow tonal, cut:
- 6 strips, 2½" x 40", for double-fold binding

*Strips are cut longer than necessary, and will be trimmed to size later.

BLOCK ASSEMBLY

1. Using 2 green #1 triangles, 1 pink #1 triangle, 1 lavender #1 triangle, 4 small-scale light #1 triangles, 1 medium-scale print #1 triangle, 1 large-scale yellow floral #1 triangle, 1 medium-scale print #2 triangle, and 1 large-scale yellow floral #2 triangle, assemble 1 block as shown. Edge-to-edge measurement of block should be 6½". Repeat to make a total of 24 blocks.

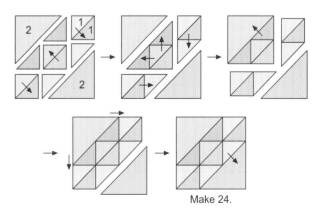

Make 24.

2. Repeat Step 1 above, doing everything the same, except using 2 purple #1 triangles instead of 2 green #1 triangles. Make 24 blocks.

QUILT TOP ASSEMBLY

1. Sew blocks together in rows, referring to the color photo in the center of the book for correct orientation of the blocks. Press seams in opposite directions from row to row.
2. Sew rows together as shown in the Quilt Assembly Diagram below. Press seams in one direction.

BORDERS

1. Measure length of quilt top through center. Cut 2 pink plaid border strips to this measurement, and sew to sides of quilt. Press seams toward border.
2. Measure width of quilt top, including borders just added, through center. Trim remaining 2 pink plaid borders strips to this measurement, and sew to top and bottom of quilt. Press seams toward border.

3. Measure length of quilt top through center. Trim 2 large-scale yellow floral border strips to this measurement, and sew to sides of quilt. Press seams toward outer border.
4. Measure width of quilt top, including borders just added, through center. Trim remaining 2 large-scale yellow floral borders strips to this measurement, and sew to top and bottom of quilt. Press seams toward outer border.

See finishing instructions on pages 34-36.

Templates

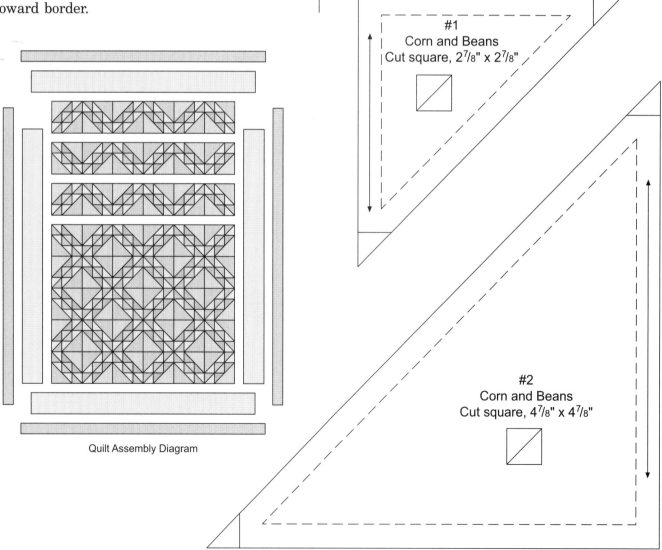

Quilt Assembly Diagram

#1
Corn and Beans
Cut square, $2^7/_8$" x $2^7/_8$"

#2
Corn and Beans
Cut square, $4^7/_8$" x $4^7/_8$"

Corn and Beans

Blossom Time

Wind Rows

Crackerbox

Crackerbox

Signature quilts, either as fund-raisers or expressions of friendship, have long been popular among women who quilt. To make this little design into a friendship quilt, replace the center #1 print rectangle in each block with a plain muslin patch and have people sign with an indelible fabric pen.

DESIGNED BY: Sharon Evans Yenter

QUILTED BY: Carrie Peterson

FINISHED QUILT SIZE: $40^{1}/_{2}$" x $52^{1}/_{2}$"

FINISHED BLOCK SIZE: $4^{1}/_{4}$" x $4^{1}/_{4}$"

See this quilt in color in the center of the book.

MATERIALS

Fabric requirements are based on Fat 8ths (useable measurement: 10" x 17"), or 40" fabric width.

- 1 Fat 8th *each* of 15 or more assorted prints for blocks
- $^{7}/_{8}$ yd. light solid for alternate squares
- 2 yds. solid green for setting triangles, border, and binding
- 3 yds. for backing (widthwise seam)
- 49" x 61" batting

Try this!

For a different look, use the Crackerbox block to make a treasured Friendship Quilt.

DIRECTIONS

See *Quiltmaking Basics,* beginning on page 2, for general cutting and piecing directions. All cutting measurements include $^{1}/_{4}$"-wide seam allowance. Press seams in direction of arrows unless otherwise instructed.

CUTTING

When a number is followed by a second number in parentheses, the first number indicates the pieces needed to make one block. The number in parentheses indicates the pieces needed to make all 48 blocks.

Study Fat 8th Cutting Diagrams below and then, from Fat 8th assortment of 15 prints, cut a total of:
- 3 (144) #1 rectangles, $1^1/2$" x $3^1/2$", for blocks
- 2 (96) squares, 3" x 3"; cut each square once diagonally to make 4 (192) #2 triangles for blocks (Trim points for easy matching, referring to the trimlines on the #2 triangle template on page 23.)

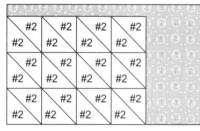

When cut as shown, one Fat 8th will yield twelve #1 rectangles, and ten #2 triangles. Do this with 12 of the Fat 8ths.

When cut as shown, one Fat 8th will yield 24 #2 triangles. Do this with the remaining 3 Fat 8ths.

From light solid, cut:
- 35 squares, $4^3/4$" x $4^3/4$", for alternate squares

From green solid, cut in order given:
- 5 strips, $2^1/2$" x 40", for double-fold binding
- 4 lengthwise strips, 50" x $2^1/2$" wide, for border (Strips are cut longer than necessary, and will be trimmed to size later.)
- 6 squares, $7^1/4$" x $7^1/4$"; cut each square twice diagonally to make 24 quarter-square side-setting #4 triangles (Trim points for easy matching, referring to the trimlines on the #4 triangle template on page 23.)
- 2 squares, $3^7/8$" x $3^7/8$"; cut each square once diagonally to make 4 half-square corner-setting #3 triangles (Trim points for easy matching, referring to the trimlines on the #3 triangle template on page 23.)

BLOCK ASSEMBLY
1. Using three #1 rectangles, assemble 1 rectangle unit as shown. Edge-to-edge measurement of unit should be $3^1/2$". Repeat to make 48 units.

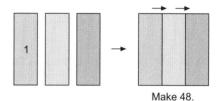

Make 48.

2. Sew four #2 triangles to rectangle unit as shown (opposite triangles should be matching prints). Edge-to-edge measurement of block should be $4^3/4$". Repeat to make 48 blocks.

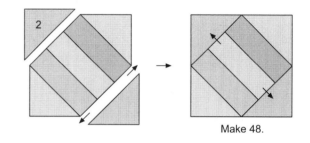

Make 48.

QUILT TOP ASSEMBLY
1. Using blocks, setting triangles, and alternate squares, make diagonal rows as shown in the Quilt Assembly Diagram on page 23. Press seams toward alternate squares and setting triangles.
2. Sew rows together. Press seams in one direction.

BORDERS
1. Measure length of quilt top through center. Cut 2 green border strips to this measurement, and sew to sides of quilt. Press seams toward border.
2. Measure width of quilt top, including borders just added, through center. Cut remaining 2 green border strips to this measurement, and sew to top and bottom of quilt. Press seam toward border.

See finishing instructions on pages 34-36.

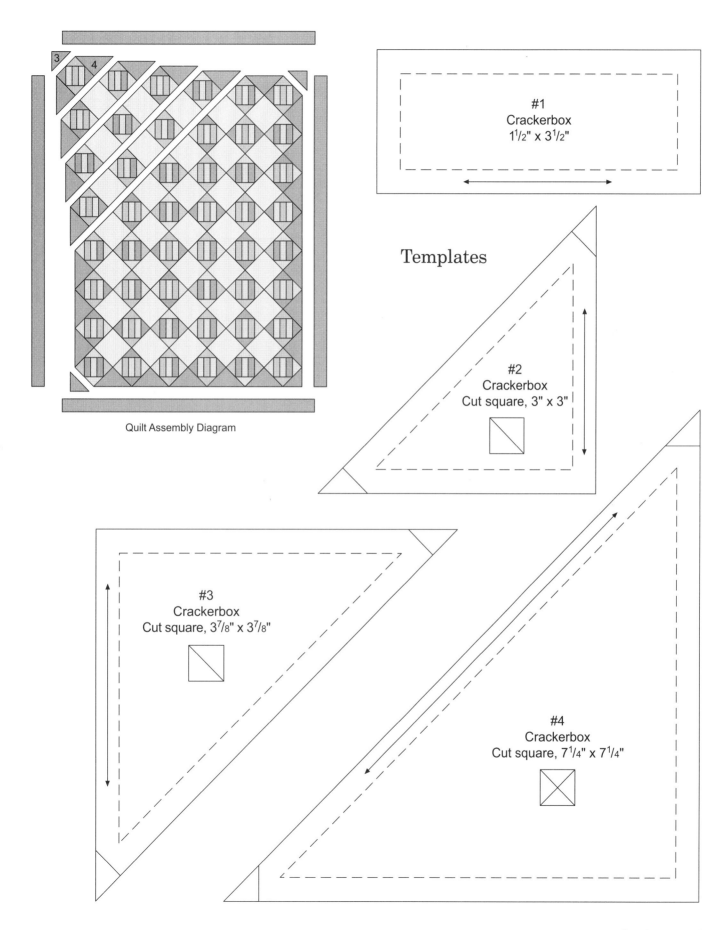

Quilt Assembly Diagram

Templates

#1
Crackerbox
$1^1/_2$" x $3^1/_2$"

#2
Crackerbox
Cut square, 3" x 3"

#3
Crackerbox
Cut square, $3^7/_8$" x $3^7/_8$"

#4
Crackerbox
Cut square, $7^1/_4$" x $7^1/_4$"

Wind Rows

These Log Cabin variation blocks are joined in what is called a Straight Furrow set. Play with the blocks once you make them, to see what other ways the lights and darks can be arranged.

DESIGNED BY: Marsha McCloskey

QUILTED BY: Linda Steller

FINISHED QUILT SIZE: $60^{1}/_{2}$" x $75^{1}/_{2}$"

FINISHED BLOCK SIZE: $7^{1}/_{2}$" x $7^{1}/_{2}$"

See this quilt in color in the center of the book.

MATERIALS

Fabric requirements are based on Fat 8ths (useable measurement: 10" x 17"), or 40" fabric width.

- 1 Fat 8th *each* of 12* or more assorted light-colored (including yellow) prints for blocks
- 1 Fat 8th *each* of 12* or more assorted purple prints for blocks
- 1 Fat 8th *each* of 4 assorted deep purple prints for blocks (we used 1 print)
- 1 Fat 8th *each* of 4 assorted green prints for blocks (we used 1 print)
- $1^{7}/_{8}$ yds. plaid for border
- $^{3}/_{4}$ yd. green tonal for binding
- 5 yds. for backing
- 69" x 84" batting

*It's fine to have some duplicates, but try to have a variety of at least 8 prints within your assortment.

DIRECTIONS

See *Quiltmaking Basics,* beginning on page 2, for general cutting and piecing directions. All cutting measurements include $^{1}/_{4}$"-wide seam allowance. Press seams in direction of arrows unless otherwise instructed.

CUTTING

When a number is followed by a second number in parentheses, the first number indicates the pieces needed to make one block. The number in parentheses indicates the pieces needed to make all 52 blocks.

Study Fat 8th Cutting Diagram below and then, from Fat 8th assortment of 12 light-colored (including yellow) prints, cut a total of:

- 1 (52) #1 squares, 2" x 2", for blocks
- 1 (52) #2 rectangles, 2" x 3½", for blocks
- 1 (52) #3 rectangles, 2" x 5", for blocks
- 1 (52) #4 rectangles, 2" x 6½", for blocks

#1	#2	#3	#4
#1	#2	#3	#4
#1	#2	#3	#4
#1	#2	#3	#4
#1	#2	#3	#4

When cut as shown, one Fat 8th will yield five #1 squares, five #2 rectangles, five #3 rectangles, and five #4 rectangles. Do this 12 times. You will have 8 extra of each piece.

Study Fat 8th Cutting Diagram above and then, from Fat 8th assortment of 12 purple prints, cut a total of:

- 1 (52) #1 squares, 2" x 2", for blocks
- 1 (52) #2 rectangles, 2" x 3½", for blocks
- 1 (52) #3 rectangles, 2" x 5", for blocks
- 1 (52) #4 rectangles, 2" x 6½", for blocks

From Fat 8th assortment of 4 deep purple prints, cut a total of:

- 5 (130) #1 squares, 2" x 2", for blocks

#1	#1	#1	#1	#1	#1	#1	#1	
#1	#1	#1	#1	#1	#1	#1	#1	
#1	#1	#1	#1	#1	#1	#1	#1	
#1	#1	#1	#1	#1	#1	#1	#1	
#1	#1	#1	#1	#1	#1	#1	#1	

When cut as shown, one Fat 8th will yield forty #1 squares. Do this 3 times. From remaining Fat 8th, cut ten #1 squares.

From Fat 8th assortment of 4 green prints, cut a total of:

- 5 (130) #1 squares, 2" x 2", for blocks

From plaid, cut:

- 4 strips, the length of fabric x 8" wide, for border (Strips are cut longer than necessary, and will be trimmed to size later.)

From green tonal, cut:

- 8 strips, 2½" x 40", for double-fold binding

BLOCK ASSEMBLY

1. Using 1 each of light-colored #1, #2, #3, and #4 pieces; 1 each of purple #1, #2, #3, and #4 pieces; and 5 green #1 squares, assemble 1 Block A as shown. Edge-to-edge measurement of block should be 8". Repeat to make a total of 26 Block A.

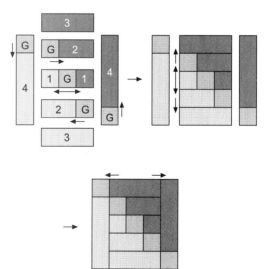

Block A
Make 26.

2. Using 1 each of light-colored #1, #2, #3, and #4 pieces; 1 each of purple #1, #2, #3, and #4 pieces; and 5 deep purple #1 squares, assemble 1 Block B as shown. Edge-to-edge measurement of block should be 8". Repeat to make a total of 26 Block B.

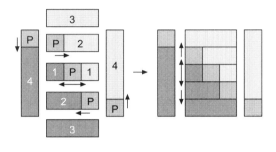

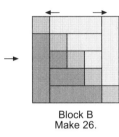

Block B
Make 26.

QUILT TOP ASSEMBLY

1. Before assembling quilt top, refer to photo in the center of the book for color placement. Then, using 24 of Block A and 24 of Block B, assemble rows as shown in the Quilt Assembly Diagram at right. Press seams in opposite directions from row to row.
2. Sew rows together. Press seams in one direction.

BORDERS

1. Measure width of quilt top through center. Cut 2 plaid border strips to this measurement. After referring to photo for placement, add a Block A and a Block B to each end of the 2 border strips. Press seams away from blocks. Set these border strips aside.
2. Measure length of quilt top through center. Cut 2 remaining plaid border strips to this measurement, and sew to sides of quilt. Press seams toward border.
3. Sew the set-aside border strips to top and bottom of quilt. Press seams toward border.

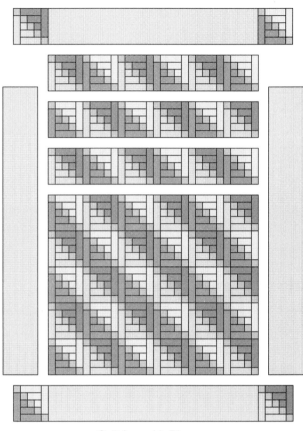

Quilt Assembly Diagram

See finishing instructions on pages 34-36.

Templates

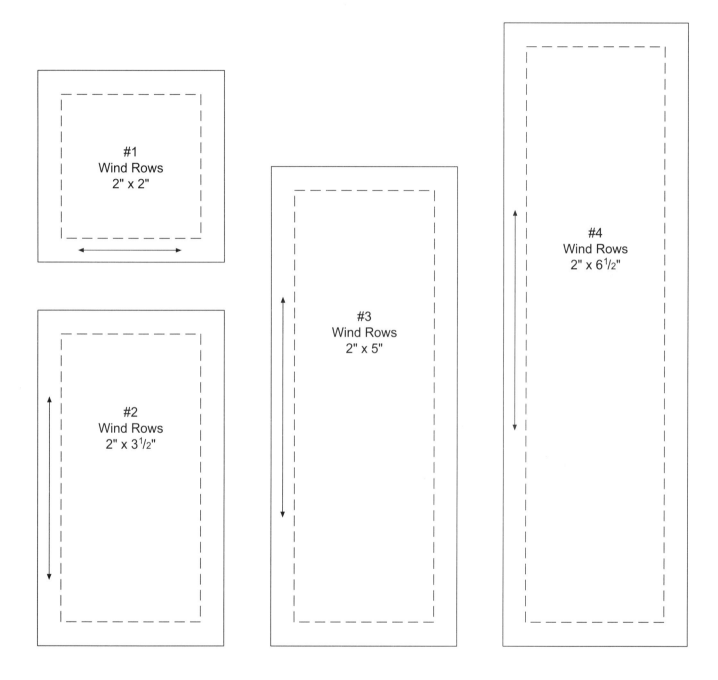

Flower Pot

Reminiscent of appliqué designs seen in newspaper patterns during the 1930s, my Flower Pots are filled with simple appliquéd posies. Making them will brighten anyone's day.

DESIGNED BY: Marsha McCloskey

QUILTED BY: Linda Steller

FINISHED QUILT SIZE: 51½" x 63½"

FINISHED BLOCK SIZE: 9" x 9"

See this quilt in color on the inside front cover.

MATERIALS

Fabric requirements are based on Fat 8ths (useable measurement: 10" x 17"), or 40" fabric width.

- 1 Fat 8th *each* of 16 or more assorted colored prints for blocks and sashing
- 1 Fat 8th green print for appliqué stems
- 1 Fat 8th *each* of 12 or more assorted light prints for blocks
- 1¾ yds. panel stripe print (4 different designs printed lengthwise on a single piece of fabric) for borders
  OR 1¾ yds. of one print
- ⅝ yd. yellow tonal for binding
- 3½ yds. for backing (widthwise seam)
- 60" x 72" batting

DIRECTIONS

See *Quiltmaking Basics,* beginning on page 2, for general cutting and piecing directions. All cutting measurements include ¼"-wide seam allowance. Press seams in direction of arrows unless otherwise instructed.

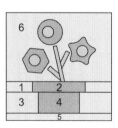

CUTTING

When a number is followed by a second number in parentheses, the first number indicates the pieces needed to make one block. The number in parentheses indicates the pieces needed to make all 12 blocks.

Note: Before cutting, please read the Paper Patch Appliqué instructions on page 30. If you are using a different appliqué method, fusing for example, you will not need to add a seam allowance when you cut the appliqué pieces.

Study Fat 8th Cutting Diagrams below and then, from Fat 8th assortment of 16 colored prints, cut a total of:

- 1 (12) #4 rectangles, $2^1/_4$" x 4", for blocks
- 1 (12) #2 rectangles, $1^3/_8$" x 5", for blocks
- 48 #8 rectangles, 2" x $9^1/_2$", for lattices
- 196 #7 squares, 2" x 2", for fourpatches and lattices
- 1 (12) of appliqué piece A
- 1 (12) of appliqué piece B
- 1 (12) of appliqué piece C
- 3 (36) of appliqué piece D

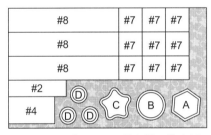

When cut as shown, one Fat 8th will yield three #8 rectangles, nine #7 squares, one #2 rectangle, one #4 rectangle, 3 of piece D, and 1 each of pieces A, B, and C. Do this with 12 of the Fat 8ths.

When cut as shown, one Fat 8th will yield 22 #7 squares, and three #8 rectangles. Do this with the remaining 4 Fat 8ths.

From Fat 8th green print, cut:

- 6 strips, $3/_4$" x 17", for appliqué stems

Study Fat 8th Cutting Diagram below and then, from Fat 8th assortment of 12 light prints, cut a total of:

- 1 (12) #6 rectangles, $6^1/_4$" x $9^1/_2$", for blocks
- 1 (12) #5 rectangles, $1^1/_8$" x $9^1/_2$", for blocks
- 2 (24) #3 rectangles, $2^1/_4$" x $3^1/_4$", for blocks
- 2 (24) #1 rectangles, $1^3/_8$" x $2^3/_4$", for blocks

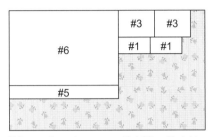

When cut as shown, one Fat 8th will yield one #6 rectangle, one #5 rectangle, two #3 rectangles, and two #1 rectangles. Do this 12 times.

From panel stripe of 4 different prints*, or from single print, cut:

- 2 strips, $3^1/_2$" x $51^1/_2$", for inner border sides
- 2 strips, $3^1/_2$" x $39^1/_2$", for inner border top and bottom
- 2 strips, $3^1/_2$" x $57^1/_2$", for outer border sides
- 2 strips, $3^1/_2$" x $45^1/_2$", for outer border top and bottom

*If using panel stripe, cut 2 strips from each of the 4 different prints.

From yellow tonal, cut:

- 7 strips, $2^1/_2$" x 40", for double-fold binding

BLOCK ASSEMBLY

1. Using your favorite appliqué technique or the one shown on page 30, appliqué flowers and stems to a #6 rectangle. Repeat to make 12 appliqué sections.

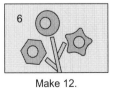

Make 12.

PAPER PATCH APPLIQUÉ

To make the flowers in the pot, you should use your favorite appliqué technique if you have one. The paper patch method described here is very traditional and works just fine. Use the ³/₄"-wide strips cut from the green Fat 8th to make the stems.

1. You'll need a paper version of each piece to be appliquéd. Trace or photocopy: 1 (12) A, 1 (12) B, 1 (12) C, 3 (36) D, 1 (12) E, 1 (12) F, and 1 (12) G.

2. Pin each paper shape to the wrong side of the fabric and add a ¹/₄" seam allowance as you cut around it.

3. To prepare the shapes for appliqué, turn the seam allowance over the paper's edge, and baste the fabric to the paper.

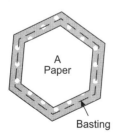

Ease fullness on curves with a small running stitch. Press.

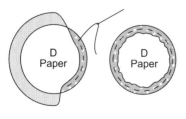

4. Determine the correct position of the appliqué shapes by placing the #6 fabric rectangle over the template in the book on page 33 and, with a pencil, lightly trace the lines of the appliqué shapes onto the fabric.

5. Leaving the paper in place, appliqué the shapes to the #6 background rectangle. Use thread the same color as the appliquéd shape. Note that stem-piece G will be sewn on after E and F. And the small D circles are sewn on after the larger flower shapes. Stitch the shapes in place by hand using a blind stitch, or by machine using a shallow zigzag stitch.

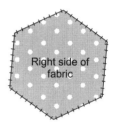

6. After each piece is stitched in place, remove the basting stitches.

7. To remove the paper, turn the block to the wrong side and carefully cut away the area behind the shapes, leaving a ¹/₄" seam allowance. Pull out the paper from the back. Press.

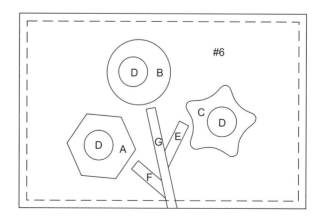

2. Using an appliqué section, and rectangles #1, #2, #3, #4, and #5, make a flower pot block as shown. Edge-to-edge measurement of block should be $9^1/_2$". Repeat to make 12 flower pot blocks.

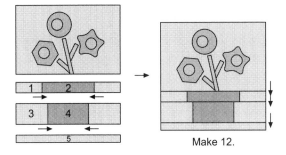

Make 12.

QUILT TOP ASSEMBLY

1. Sew 2 assorted colored print #8 rectangles together as shown. Edge-to-edge measurement of unit should be $3^1/_2$" x $9^1/_2$". Repeat to make 24 lattice strip units.

8
8

Make 24.

2. Using 12 assorted colored print #7 squares, assemble a unit as shown. Edge-to-edge measurement of unit should be $3^1/_2$" x $9^1/_2$". Repeat to make 7 of these lattice square units.

Make 7.

3. Sew 4 assorted colored print #7 squares together as shown. Edge-to-edge measurement of fourpatch should be $3^1/_2$". Repeat to make 28 of these fourpatches.

Make 28.

4. Using blocks, lattice strip units, lattice square units, and 20 fourpatches (8 remaining fourpatches will be used for borders), assemble rows as shown in the Quilt Assembly Diagram at right. Press seams toward lattice units.

5. Sew rows together. Press seams in one direction.

BORDERS

1. Inner border: sew the two $3^1/_2$" x $51^1/_2$" border strips to sides of quilt. Press seams toward border. Sew a fourpatch to each end of the two $3^1/_2$" x $39^1/_2$" border strips. Press seams away from fourpatches. Sew these border strips to top and bottom of quilt. Press seams toward border.

2. Outer border: sew the two $3^1/_2$" x $57^1/_2$" border strips to sides of quilt. Press seams toward outer border. Sew a fourpatch to each end of the two $3^1/_2$" x $45^1/_2$" border strips. Press seams away from fourpatches. Sew these border strips to top and bottom of quilt. Press seams toward outer border.

Quilt Assembly Diagram

See finishing instructions on pages 34-36.

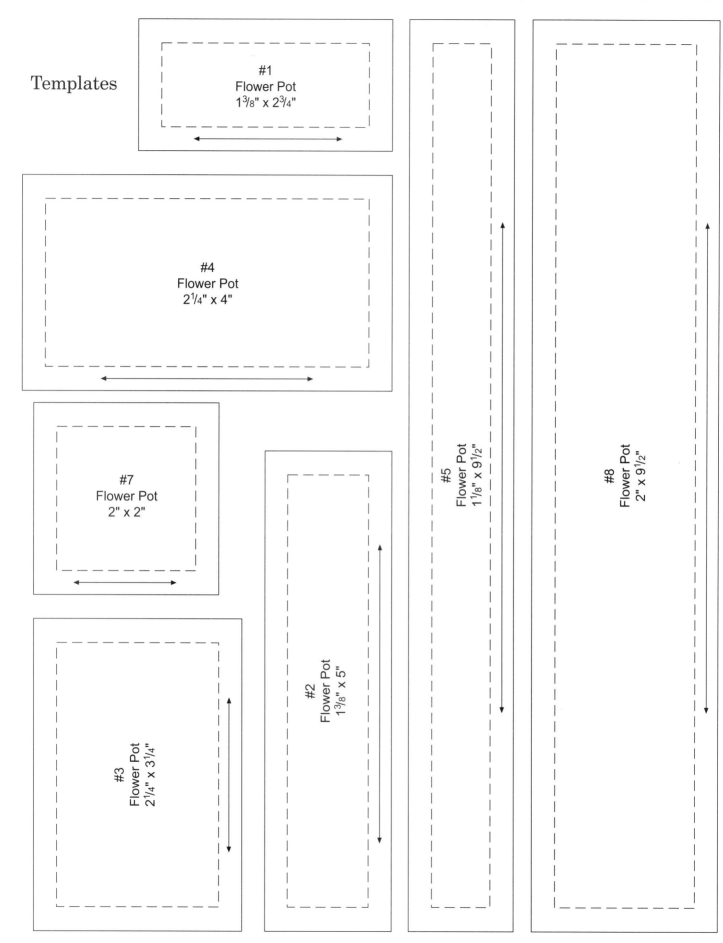

Templates

#1
Flower Pot
1³/₈" x 2³/₄"

#4
Flower Pot
2¹/₄" x 4"

#7
Flower Pot
2" x 2"

#3
Flower Pot
2¹/₄" x 3¹/₄"

#2
Flower Pot
1³/₈" x 5"

#5
Flower Pot
1¹/₈" x 9¹/₂"

#8
Flower Pot
2" x 9¹/₂"

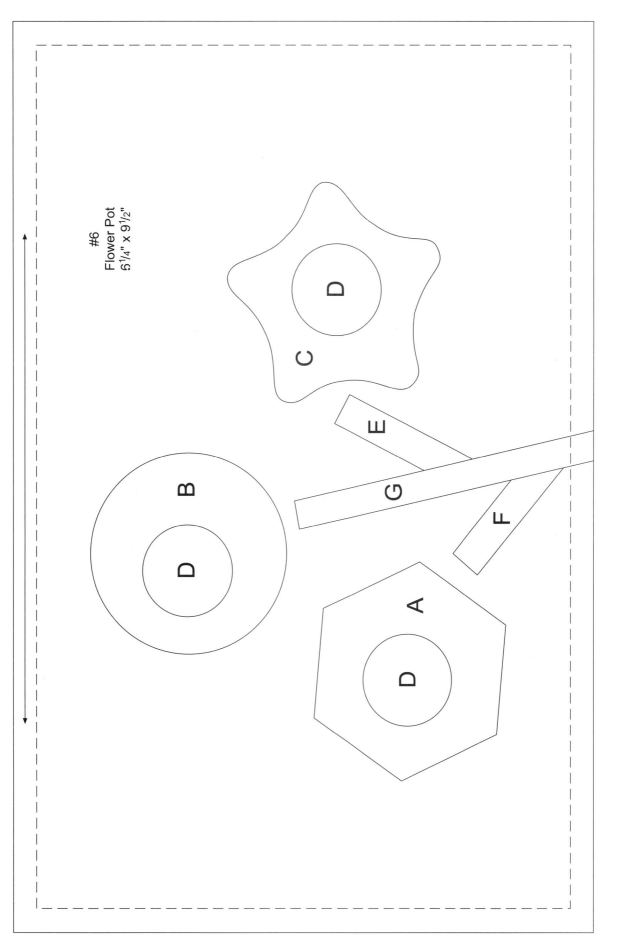

#6
Flower Pot
6¼" x 9½"

C

D

B

D

E

G

F

A

D

Quiltmaking Basics

MAKING YOUR QUILT TOP

Setting the Quilt Blocks Together

When the design blocks and setting pieces (large squares, triangles and/or lattice strips) are sewn together to make a quilt top, it is called the "set." Each quilt pattern has a Quilt Assembly Diagram showing how the parts will be sewn together in rows. Sometimes the rows go across the quilt and sometimes on the diagonal. When sewing the rows together, press for opposing seams and pin all points of matching.

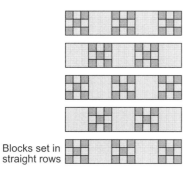

Blocks set in
straight rows

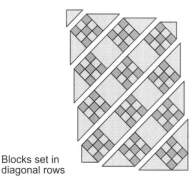

Blocks set in
diagonal rows

Borders

The borders for the quilts in this book are made of strips of fabric sewn to the sides and then to the top and bottom edges of the quilt top. Some of the borders have pieced blocks at the corners.

To cut the two side borders to the right length, measure the quilt top length (including seam allowances) through the center. (On large quilts, it's a good idea to measure the length along both outer edges as well and use the average of the three measurements.) Cut the two strips this length. Mark the center and quarter points on both the quilt top and border strips. Matching ends, centers, and quarter points, pin border strips to the quilt top. Pin generously and press along the matched edges to set the seam before sewing. A shot of steam will help with any easing that might be required.

Using a $1/4$" seam allowance, stitch the border to the quilt top. Press the seam allowance to one side as directed in the quilt instructions. For the top and bottom borders, measure the quilt width, including the borders just added. Cut the strips. Add necessary corner blocks, if any, and attach the two border strips.

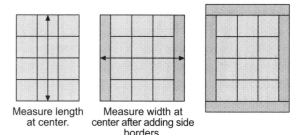

Measure length
at center.

Measure width at
center after adding side
borders.

FINISHING YOUR QUILT

Plan and Mark Quilting Designs

The fabrics used in *Fat 8ths and Friends* make a lively quilt surface in design and color. Frankly, too many fancy quilting designs on these quilts would be a waste of effort because you couldn't see them. All of our quilts were quilted by machine with simple designs to complement our simple piecing.

Quilting lines should be evenly distributed over the quilt surface. Directions that come with your batting will tell how close the quilting lines must be to keep the batting from coming apart when the quilt is washed. Avoid tight complicated designs that then require similar quilting over the whole quilt. Likewise avoid leaving large areas unquilted.

Some quilters prefer to mark their quilt top with quilting lines before it is assembled with the backing and batting. To do this, you will need marking pencils, a long ruler or yardstick; stencils or templates for quilting motifs; and a smooth, clean, hard surface on which to work. Thoroughly press the quilt top. Use a sharp marking pencil and lightly mark the quilting lines on the fabric.

No matter what kind of marking tool you use, light lines will be easier to remove than heavy ones.

Backing and Batting

Prepare the backing. For quilts that measure more than 38" wide, you will need to make the backing by cutting and sewing two or more lengths of fabric together. Add 8" to the length and width of the completed quilt top for a working allowance (4" all the way around).

To make a backing that is large enough, cut lengths of fabric and sew them together on the long sides. Press the seams open. You can sew two lengths together with one center seam, or split the second length and sew the pieces to each side of the other length of fabric. Sometimes, to save fabric, it is best to cut and piece the backing so the seam runs across the width of the quilt.

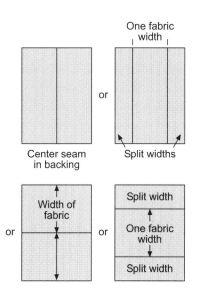

Choose a thin cotton or cotton-polyester blend batting in a size that is longer and wider than your quilt top. Trim batting to size of backing.

Layering the Quilt

Lay the backing face down on a large, clean, flat surface – the floor or a large table. With masking tape, tape the backing down to keep it smooth and flat while you are working with the other layers. If you are working on a table, part of the quilt will probably hang over the sides. Begin in the quilt center and work in sections toward the sides and ends. Gently lay the batting on top of the backing,

centering and smoothing it as you go. Center the freshly ironed quilt top on top of the batting, right side up. Starting in the middle, gently smooth out fullness to the sides and corners. Take care not to distort the straight lines of the quilt design and the borders.

Baste the layers together with safety pins or needle and light-colored thread. Start in the middle and make a line of long stitches to each corner to form a large X. Continue basting in a grid of parallel lines 6"-8" apart. Finish with a row of basting around the outside edges – $1/4$" away from the edge.

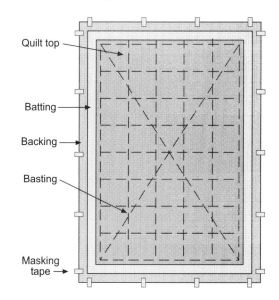

Quilting

Quilt the layers together by hand or machine. This is a little sentence to cover a big subject. There are whole books written on how to quilt. There are also many machine-quilting services that will do the quilting for you. Before you decide on a quilting method, consider how you will be using your quilt. Will it be a rarely-used heirloom quilt, or do you plan to use the quilt daily? Heirloom quilts are often enhanced by hand-quilting. Everyday quilts may be better served by quick and durable machine quilting.

Binding

After quilting, trim excess batting and backing even with the edge of the quilt top. A rotary cutter and long ruler will ensure accurate straight edges. If basting is no longer in place, baste all three layers of the quilt together close to the edge.

Cut binding strips 2½" wide, either with the straight grain of the fabric or on the bias. With right sides together, join the strips as shown. Make enough continuous binding to go around the four sides of the quilt plus 6" to 10" for overlap.

Joining straight-cut binding strips.

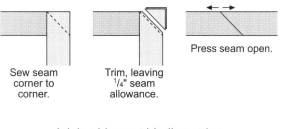

Sew seam corner to corner. Trim, leaving ¼" seam allowance. Press seam open.

Joining bias-cut binding strips.

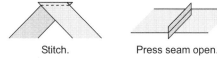

Stitch. Press seam open.

Fold the binding in half lengthwise with wrong sides together and press, taking care not to stretch it. At one end, open out the fold and turn the raw edge in at a 45° angle. Press. Trim, leaving a ¼" seam allowance.

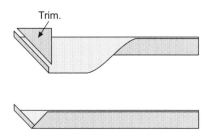

Trim.

Beginning on one edge of the quilt a few inches from a corner, pin the binding to the quilt top. Beginning two inches from the folded end of the binding, stitch ⅜" from the raw edges and stop ⅜" from the raw edge at the corner. Backstitch and remove the quilt.

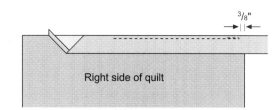

⅜"

Right side of quilt

Fold the binding back on itself to create a 45° angle, then turn the binding down to make a fold in the binding that is in line with the upper raw edge of the quilt top. Pin. Stitch the binding to the quilt, ending ⅜" from the next corner. Backstitch and miter the corner as you did the previous one.

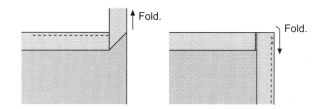

Fold. Fold.

Continue in this manner until the binding has been stitched to all four edges of the quilt top. When you reach the beginning of the binding, trim away excess, leaving 1" to tuck into the folded binding. Complete the stitching. Turn the binding to the back of the quilt and hand sew in place, mitering corners as shown.

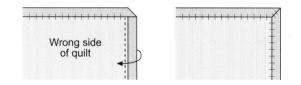

Wrong side of quilt